How To
Bench BIG

12-Week Bench Press Program

&

Technique Guide

By

Ryan J. Mathias

MathiasMethod.com

COPYRIGHT

DISCLAIMER

ABOUT THE AUTHOR

Ryan J. Mathias

Hi,

I'm Ryan Mathias, creator of the Mathias Method Strength System and for years I have been helping people all over the world, from total beginners to elite athletes, learn how to get stronger, perform better, and achieve their goals.

As an athlete, Strength Coach and competitive Powerlifter with 10+ years of experience, all backed by a Degree in Exercise Science, I have taken my experience and combined it with my education to bring you the best and most effective knowledge available.

I share everything I know in my books and it is my goal to help as many people as I can learn how to achieve their goals. Because I measure my success not by how many books I sell, but by how many people I help.

So, if you want to learn how to get bigger, stronger, faster, and overall perform better, then I'm your guy!

Plus, if you ever have any questions, you can email me anytime and I will do my best to help you reach your goals!

Email: ryan@mathiasmethod.com
I would love to hear from you!

Join me on Social Media: @RyanJMathias

BOOKS BY RYAN J. MATHIAS

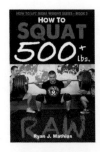   

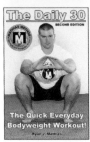   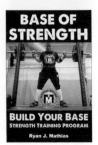

Available on

Amazon.com

and

StrengthWorld.store

DEDICATION

This information is dedicated to you, the lifter. To those of you that believe in becoming stronger. Stronger through self-improvement and the pursuit of greater achievement. For those that always push for more and crave success every day. For those that don't let challenges stop them from doing what they set out to do. For all the dreamers out there, that keep their dreams alive!

This information is dedicated to YOU, because YOU are the only one that can make a difference in your life. YOU are the only one that can change YOUR world!

THANK YOU

Thank you to all those that read this information and use it to help others. My mission is to help as many people as I can change the world through strength and I know I can't do it alone. So, thank you for standing with me.

TABLE OF CONTENTS

PART 1

INTRODUCTION

A NOTE FROM THE AUTHOR

Hey Lifter!

I hope you are ready to get really strong, because you are about to embark on an incredible Strength Journey! The same journey that I followed when I first started! The journey to get stronger!

If you are like me, wanting to Bench BIG, but fighting just to gain a few pounds of strength after months of training, I feel you! I've been there. I to struggle with the bench press and always have.

For a long time I was one of those people that hated the bench press, even to the point where I just wouldn't do it. I didn't understand the lift and I was not very good at it. Eventually, I moved past my negativity and, despite my troubles, made the goal to one day bench BIG weight.

I started all over again, going through all the trouble of perfecting the technique and learning the best way to bench BIG. Now my bench is no longer a weakness of mine! It is a strength!

However, it wasn't easy for me to get there. I had to fight for every single pound of strength I got! Which is why I made this book. To give you an easier path to finally discover how to Bench BIG weight!

In fact, I created the entire *How To Lift More Weight* series for all the Strength Warriors out there that are just like us, looking to get stronger! I really want to help others, achieve their goals of lifting as much weight as they can dream of in all their lifts!

Just remember, it won't be easy. You are gonna have to work for it. I am giving you all the tools you need to succeed, but the rest is up to you.

Before you get started, I want you to realize that no ordinary person has ever completed this Journey. That is because in order to reach such an incredible strength feat, you cannot be ordinary. You have to develop yourself into someone that has character, focus and strength beyond the ordinary. You will have to become extraordinary in your efforts to defeat the challenging road that lays ahead.

You will have to be consistent, dedicated and self-disciplined enough to persevere to the end. You can have others join in along your journey, but YOU must be the one that keeps fighting until the end. No one can do it for you. You have to be the one that decides to not give up and push on no matter how hard it gets.

I cannot promise that you will reach your goal, but I will guarantee that this program will guide you as far as you want to go. The rest is up to you. Are you ready?

Strength To You,

Ryan J. Mathias

Go to MathiasMethod.com to learn about my Strength Journey!

The Definition Of RAW

Now let's start off with a definition of what we powerlifters consider a lift to be done "RAW".

"RAW" determines the assistance you are allowed to use for training and testing your lifts. What we consider to be RAW in this book is the same as what most sanctioned Powerlifting Competitions also consider to be RAW.

This is different than what is considered to be 100% RAW. 100% RAW means without any assistive equipment at all, as if you were only lifting in shorts and a t-shirt.

For this program we allow for some safety equipment to accommodate more people and promote safety of the lifter, above all else.

To be considered RAW you can use the assistance of:

- ☑ **a weight lifting belt,**

- ☑ **non-supportive elbow sleeves,**

- ☑ **chalk as needed,**

- ☑ **and wrist wraps if needed.**

Non-supportive elbow sleeves are used to promote joint safety by keeping the elbows warm, but should add little to no actual lifting support.

This amount of equipment promotes safety of the lifter while allowing for only necessary assistance. Overall, the lifter has to do the lift, not the equipment.

The more equipment you use, the more you have to rely on for max day. It is best to only use what you need to be safe and save the rest for when you absolutely need it.

Drugs and Supplements

Being RAW also does not allow the use of drugs or special supplement regiments that greatly improve a lifter's strength, recovery or muscle growth. Basically, if you would fail a drug test using it, then it is not RAW.

To be clear, no supplements are needed to make this program work as effectively as possible. End of story.

LIFTING EQUIPMENT

Lifting equipment is anything that directly improves your ability to lift more weight. This could be very light assistive gear, such as knee or elbow sleeves, all the way up to extremely supportive gear, such as lifting suits.

One of the most common pieces of equipment to use during the bench press is wrist wraps. When used properly, wrist wraps help you to keep your wrists straight and, therefore, transfer more energy into the bar as you press. They are also great for decreasing wrist pain when you are lifting heavy. These are great to use when you need to take some pressure off your wrists, but need to be limited. If you are not benching over 350 pounds, you really don't need them.

Chalk is another common lifting tool that is always permitted, as needed, and can help you both grip the bar and stick to the bench better, but only use it if you need it for extra support. Apply a light amount to your palms to improve your grip and/or have someone rub it on your upper trapezius muscles where you press into the bench to prevent sliding while you lift heavy.

Equipment can improve lifter strength and safety, but can also have adverse effects when used improperly.

If any one piece of equipment is used too frequently, then it will limit your body's ability to grow stronger in that area. Essentially, the equipment will become a crutch that then must be used every time training occurs in order to keep up with the strength developed in other non-supported areas.

The most effective way to use equipment is only when it is necessary. For example, when using light to moderate loads (<75%) avoid using any equipment at all to build greater strength in all areas. Then when you put on equipment for maximal loads (>80%) you will be that much stronger.

Even if you have an injury, only use the equipment when you need it. If your injury does not hurt, then do not cover it up with equipment. Allow it to grow stronger.

When you are building strength, use little to no equipment.

When you are testing strength, use whatever you can to improve your lift.

THE BENCH PRESS

The Bench Press is the absolute best lift for both building and testing your upper body strength. It is an extremely valuable training tool that builds your upper body like no other lift can. If you have a BIG Bench, then your entire upper body is well developed!

Like most lifts, the bench press is a lift where some people love it and some hate it. Those that hate it, are usually the ones that don't understand it and do it wrong. However, if you learn how to do it right, it can be just as good as any of your other lifts.

With that said, there are 3 important things you need to know about the bench press before you can start benching BIG.

First, the bench press is NOT just an upper body lift.

Though it focuses on your upper body, you must use your entire body as one unit to lift the most weight safe and effectively. The biggest part of this is simply setting up in a position that puts the least amount of stress on your shoulders and helps you to maintain stability as you lift.

Most problems with the bench press come from simply not setting up in the proper position to lift from, resulting in instability while you lift and high shoulder stress. The body was simply not made to hold a heavy load with our arms shoved back behind our bodies, and then have to press it away. That is why it is so important to learn how to lift correctly, so you stay safe while training to get brutally strong!

Next, the key to a BIG Bench is strong triceps!

The Bench Press is a triceps dominant lift, not a "chest exercise". Let me say that again...it doesn't matter how much you can do pec flyes with, because the triceps do most of the work in the bench press. That is true for any pressing move we do.

It doesn't matter if you are doing wide grip or closegrip. Your chest and shoulders work together as stabilizers that only do some of the actual lift, while the triceps do all of the arm extension, or pressing work.

The reason the bench press is often considered a "chest exercise" is because your chest is the weakest link in the chain. Whatever is weakest, gets fatigued first and therefore builds up. However, the stronger muscles do that actual lifting.

Same goes for military press. Your triceps do the work, but your shoulders feel it because they are the weakest link that fatigues first.

For a BIG Bench, your entire upper body needs to be strong, but strong triceps are key! Everything else will catch up to them as you train more.

Third, the stronger your back is the stronger your bench press will be.

Having a strong back plays a HUGE roll in counteracting all the big presses you do. Not only that, but your back strength helps to keep your shoulders healthy so you can bench safely and more often. If you have a strong back you can stabilize yourself and the weight better leading to BIG numbers, fast! So make sure you do a ton of back work whenever you can!

Apply these things and you will be well on your way to benching BIG! Now lets's go bench!

DO PUSH-UPS DAILY

The push-up is a great way to both learn proper bench press technique and start off your strength training career.

If you cannot do push-ups with perfect form, then you are not ready to lift weights. Strength training starts with your own bodyweight and only when your own bodyweight is not enough should you progress to weight training.

That is the same for kids, teens and adults. Except for extreme cases, everyone needs to be able to do push-ups first.

In fact, you should be doing push-ups daily! No matter how much you can already lift, push-ups are the perfect exercise to do everyday! They will actually help with recovery and make you even stronger!

That is why I created the *Daily 30*, which is a quick everyday bodyweight exercise routine made specifically for those that want to get stronger and recover faster. This routine has you doing a quick 2 minute bodyweight workout at least once per day to help you build even more strength, decrease muscle and joint pain, and improve your recovery between workouts.

If you have shoulder pain, or any muscular problems, you are definitely gonna want to get this! To learn more about the *Daily 30* go to my website MathiasMethod.com and start getting even stronger by doing push-ups everyday!

BENCH PRESS FOR BEGINNERS

How we teach the bench press to a beginner is different than how we teach it to a more advanced lifter. This is because beginners are still figuring out their body's leverages and what works best for them while an advanced lifter knows what does and does not work for them based on experience.

When you are just starting out and discovering how your body moves with weight in your hands, begin by doing what is comfortable. Grab the bar where it is comfortable, set up how it is comfortable, bring the bar down to your chest where it is comfortable, and press up however it is comfortable. From there you can start making minor adjustments to see what works best for you.

Try to continuously improve your technique, while maintaining control of the weight and not letting the weight control you.

If you need to change something then make small changes. Remember, small changes make a big difference, so do not go from a wide grip to a super close grip. Start with slight adjustments and see how it feels before changing more.

Realize that things are going to take some time. Just be patient and soon enough you will be benching like a pro!

Overall, beginners should focus on the basics and getting the general movement down before trying to apply every detail. The details will come. After benching for a while you'll start to feel what works better for you versus someone else, and as your body changes, so too will your technique. Focus on strength first, and improve your technique over time.

BENCH PRESS FOR ADVANCED LIFTERS

Advanced lifters are those that have been benching for over a year and have developed a strong base of strength. If you have not been benching for at least this long, I highly recommend you start with my *Base Of Strength Program* (see page 6) to build up all 3 of your base lifts while getting a lot of bench press practice in.

Also, any beginners you know should start off with that program before advancing to the advanced program in this book.

When benching, an advanced lifter should be specific and focus on the details while their subconscious does the most basic aspects of the lift for them. This means taking a quick moment before every single lift to go through a checklist of specifics you need to perfect your technique.

THE BENCH PRESS CHECKLIST

After you set-up and pull the weight out, take a quick moment to check:

- ☑ **Are you crushing the bar in your hands?**
- ☑ **Are your shoulders tucked back and down?**
- ☑ **Is your chest high and back tight?**
- ☑ **Are your feet pressed into the ground?**
- ☑ **Is your core braced; front, back and sides?**
- ☑ **Are you driving your head back into the bench?**
- ☑ **Are you confident and focused on your lift?**

If you can answer "Yes" to all of these questions, then you are perfectly set to bench BIG. The next step is to perfect your lifting technique.

The thing is, the bench press is a lift that is never perfect and needs constant tweaking. You can always move smoother. You can always drive harder. You can always brace tighter. There is always something to improve and focus on.

With every workout, try to focus on one or two aspects of your technique to perfect. If you need help, asking a knowledgeable friend or trainer can really help. They can give you feedback both during your set and immediately after to help you see what needs to improve.

If you don't have that option, you can always record yourself. Just try to video from multiple angles to make sure no technique issues are hiding from the camera angle you chose.

You can also ask me anytime! You can tag me on Instagram @MathiasMethod or Facebook @MathiasMethodStrength asking for some tips and I would be happy to take a look at your lifts!

If we don't get back to you within day, then you can always message us or try my personal account @RyanJMathias. I am active on all accounts daily, but I am also a busy guy. I will get to as many as I can as often as I can, so please be patient with me if the response is not immediate.

Just remember, your bench press is NEVER going to be perfect! There is always something to improve! If you are not improving, then you are limiting your full potential.

Now let's find what you need to improve and go bench!

BENCH PRESS PRINCIPLES

All proper bench press technique will have the same principles, no matter your grip or hand position, that must be followed for safe and effective technique. These principles are presented below.

- ☑ **The bar is always in line with your wrists and elbows.**

- ☑ **The bar touches your chest for a full range of motion.**

- ☑ **Your shoulders stay tucked with your chest high.**

- ☑ **Hips stay down on the bench.**

- ☑ **Feet do not move during the entire lift.**

   These Bench Press Principles apply to all variations.

Any bench press that follows these principles is a perfect lift! Speed is not important. Technique and control of the weight is.

Beyond these principles, there are two main variables that can change how a bench looks and is used. These are your grip and foot position.

CHOOSING YOUR BENCH GRIP

Hand position will vary for every individual.

The goal is to place your hands where you will be in the most safe and effective position to lift the most weight.

A closer grip increases the range of motion and focuses more tension on your triceps, while a wider grip decreases the range of motion and emphasizes more on your shoulders and chest.

If you have strong triceps (arms), you may want to try a medium grip and tuck your elbows in while you lift. If you have a strong chest and shoulders, then you may prefer a wider grip with only a slight elbow tuck. The triceps are the prime mover for the bench press so a super wide grip is not usually optimal for strength.

Choose the grip that best utilizes your leverages.

Also, when grabbing the bar, it is best to always wrap your thumbs around the bar. Thumbless Benching, known as Suicide Grip, is not wrong, but it is dangerous (hence the name) and prevents you from getting the proper shoulder tightness by externally rotating your hands on the bar.

Note: For beginners, just grab the bar where it feels comfortable and adjust from there as your technique develops.

CHOOSING YOUR FOOT POSITION

Your feet are your base point and create stability as you lift.

Your feet can be placed anywhere that gives you the greatest amount of stability, or leg drive, while keeping your hips down on the bench during the entire lift. This can be with your feet flat or on the balls of your feet.

The ultimate goal of foot placement should be to get your knee lower than your hip so that you can get the most leg drive without losing position, or tightness, throughout your body.

If your knee is equal too or higher than your hip when sitting on the bench with your feet flat and shins vertical, then you will need to tuck your feet back under towards your hips during your set-up so that your knees drop below hip level. The degree of tuck under is up to you and the more you tuck them the higher your heel will raise off the floor.

This position also requires a good amount of hip flexor mobility, so make sure that you work on stretching your hip flexors often.

If your knee is lower than your hip when sitting on the bench with your feet flat and shins vertical, then you should place your feet directly under your knees. You can tuck them more, but this will not get you anymore leg drive.

The more your foot is in contact with the ground, the greater leg drive you will have.

Note: *For beginners, just place your feet where it is comfortable. You can adjust from there over time.*

PART 2

PERFECTING YOUR TECHNIQUE

Bench Press Technique Guide

The Ultimate Bench Press Guide

This one-of-a-kind Bench Press Guide gives you all the tools you need to bench more weight than ever!

- ☑ **Breathing and Bracing Techniques**

- ☑ **Proper Set-Up**

- ☑ **How To Unrack**

- ☑ **Proper Lifting Technique**

- ☑ **Technique Checklist**

- ☑ **Common Mistakes and How To Correct Them**

- ☑ **Top Accessory Exercises**

- ☑ **Bench Press Variations**

- ☑ **Tips and Tricks**

- ☑ **and even How To Spot Properly**

Read on to start building your strongest bench press ever!

BENCH PRESS

PURPOSE

- • **Test Upper Body Strength**

- • **Build Upper Body Strength**

PRIME MOVERS

- • **Triceps** (Arms)

- • **Anterior Deltoid** (Shoulders)

- • **Pectoralis Major** (Chest)

HOW TO BENCH PRESS STRONGER

BREATHING AND BRACING

How you breathe during the bench press can greatly influence your pressing strength.

What you may have been taught before is to breathe in as you bring the bar down and breathe out as you press back up. This is good if you are in a cardio class using extremely light weights, and just need to keep your endurance up, but if you are looking to get stronger this is one of the worst things you can do.

By breathing in as you descend, your body is not as tight as it can be, and is, therefore, unstable. It is similar too doing a bench press while laying on an exercise ball versus on a solid bench. The more stable you are, the more you can lift. So you need to think more about how you are going to breathe during your lift than what people do for general fitness.

If you want to get stronger, or build muscle, then you need to lift heavy, and to lift heavy you need to have your body braced as tightly as possible to have the most strength for your lift. For that you should use what is called the Valsalva Maneuver, which promotes the greatest amount of strength by increasing your spine stabilization through increased intra-abdominal pressure and raising your chest. The two versions of this are described next.

VALSALVA MANEUVER

Suck in as much air as you can and hold it in, attempting to raise your chest and create as much intra-abdominal pressure as you can, to stabilize your spine. Then press your lips closed to hold the air in while flexing all of the musculature surrounding your entire torso, and forcing the air deep down into your abdomen.

Think of your torso as a soda can you are trying to fill up and pressurize. You have your pelvic floor as the base, your diaphragm as the top, and all your abdominal (front, back and side) musculature making the outer walls of the can. You want to fill the can with air and flex everything around it as tight as possible to keep the air in.

A lifting belt can help with this, but make sure that you do not tighten it too much or you will not be able to get a full breath and raise your chest as high. Always keep your belt loose enough so that you can put just the 4 fingers of your hand down into the belt against your stomach with ease. Then when you brace you want to think of bracing out against the belt so that it gets filled up tightly and your fingers can no longer fit in.

The valsalva maneuver greatly increases your blood pressure and should only be held for 1-2 maximal repetitions, or when you are using over 90% of your maximum. Sets with more than 1-3 reps, or under 90% of your maximum should use the Partial Valsalva Maneuver.

PARTIAL VALSALVA MANEUVER

This is the same as the Valsalva Maneuver, except you exhale after getting past the sticking point of the lift. This helps to decrease the overall blood pressure increase created by the pressure and allows for more fluid reps to be performed, while still having a very strong lift.

For the bench press, suck in as much air as you can and brace tightly just before taking the weight out of the rack. Hold this air as you get set, then suck in again to brace harder just before you start to bring the weight down.

Hold your breathe while you bring the weight down and pause on your chest, then start to breathe out, while still bracing your core, after you have made it about half way up from the bottom, or just past your sticking point.

Then breathe in again before every rep to re-brace.

SET-UP

The set-up is all about getting your body into the strongest position to lift the most amount of weight, safely and efficiently.

Basically, it is all about tightness. You have to create tension in the right places without wasting energy and maintain it during the entire lift. If you lose tightness, then you lose strength.

Take your time and make it perfect. If anything is off, then reset and do it again.

LAY FLAT ON THE BENCH

Start by lying down completely flat, with your feet set on the end of the bench.

SET YOUR HANDS

After finding your preferred width, evenly set according to the power rings, spread your fingers as wide as you can as if to engulf as much of the bar in your hand as possible.

Then grasp the bar tightly with your thumbs wrapped, trying to crush the bar in your hands to take control of the weight, while keeping your wrists straight.

This is your control point, SO TAKE CONTROL!!! Make the weight feel small while you become invincible with your crushing grip!

Note: Every barbell is slightly different. NEVER base your grip on the knurling of the bar. ALWAYS base your grip off of the Power Rings in the knurling, even if you are like me and have your grip about 1 inch inside the rings. Though some cheaper barbells have their power rings in closer than competition barbells, it is still a much better way to base your grip. If all else fails, just close your eyes and grab the bar where it is comfortable and adjust from their as needed.

SET YOUR SHOULDERS

Press your feet down into the bench to raise your hips high, then pull your shoulders up off the bench while creating an external rotation torque with your hands, also known as bending the bar. Pull your shoulder blades back, together, and down towards your hips.

Next, firmly press your upper trapezius down into the bench, while keeping your shoulders tucked. Your eyes should be in line with the bar.

This is all meant to create an arch in your chest, not your lower back. Keep your chest high, and shoulders together during the entire lift.

SET YOUR HIPS

While maintain tension, and an arch in your chest, set your hips down on the bench, to where your chest is as high as you can get it.

SET YOUR FEET

With your hips in place, set one foot at a time down on the floor, while pressing down and out to maintain tension throughout your entire body. Think as if you are trying to slide your toes to the front of your shoe while pressing down hard into the ground.

Make sure your feet are set in a place where your knees are below your hips and your hips can stay on the bench, even when you push down harder. If you are having difficulty with this you need to work on your hip flexor mobility. You can do that by following my How To Warm-Up Guide.

To maintain tension throughout your entire body as you lift, brace your core, press your knees out hard to engage your glutes and keep your feet pressed into the ground.

After you are set-up absolutely NOTHING should move during the entire lift other than your arms. No opening and closing of hands, no foot wiggles, no movement at all. If you do get out of place, start all over until you get it right.

Unrack

Brace Your Core

Suck in as much air as you can and hold it in, attempting to create as much intra-abdominal pressure as you can, to stabilize your spine. Then press your lips closed to hold the air in while flexing all of the musculature surrounding your entire torso, and forcing the air deep down into your abdomen. This is known as the Valsalva Maneuver.

Hold this air in tight as you lift only breathing as needed between reps.

Pull The Bar Out

While maintaining full body tightness and an external rotation torque on the bar, lock your arms to lift the bar only slightly over the bench hooks and pull the bar out until it is over your shoulders. Again, arms should be locked with your chest high and shoulders back and down.

Make sure that you get your lats tight as you pull the bar out as well, to help you stabilize the entire lift, allowing you to lift more.

Note: No matter the weight, it is best to do this with a spotter handing you the bar to maintain proper shoulder position. Do not shrug your shoulders forward to lift the weight out.

THE BENCH PRESS

The bench press is as simple as pulling the weight down to your chest to create back tightness, then pressing yourself down into the bench as you extend your arms to lockout.

Make sure that you rotate your elbows in as you bring the weight down to limit shoulder strain, then flare your elbows out as you press for a stronger lift. This both saves energy for when you need it to press and keeps your shoulders safe.

PULL THE BAR DOWN DOWN

While keeping your wrist straight and chest as high as possible, initiate the downward motion by pulling the bar down onto your chest, with your elbows tucked in slightly towards your sides, and engaging your lats.

PAUSE ON YOUR CHEST

Touch the bar to your chest and pause, without it bouncing. Your elbows should be directly under the bar and range from a 30-45 degree angle from your sides.

Find the best position for you, and if you have shoulder or torso mobility problems you should try to improve them before every training session. You can do this with my How To Warm-Up Guide.

PRESS INTO THE BENCH

Press your traps down into the bench, while keeping your chest as high as possible, and flare your elbows out as you press the bar up and back over your shoulders where the lift began.

The more you press down into the bench, the stronger your press will be!

KEY POINTS

☑ Crush the bar in your hands and keep your wrists straight.

☑ Chest high with your shoulders tucked back and down.

☑ Keep your hips down on the bench with your knees lower than your hips for more pressing power.

☑ Press your feet into the ground with no wiggles.

☑ Keep your entire body tight so only your arms move during the entire lift.

☑ Control the entire range of motion.

☑ Tuck your elbows slightly when you pull the bar down (for shoulder safety).

☑ Flare your elbows out when you press (for a stronger press).

Always use spotters during your lifts for safety.

COMMON BENCH PRESS MISTAKES

IMPROPER SET-UP

Make sure that everything is perfect before you start. If you set-up wrong, then your entire lift is going to be wrong.

You can't correct your position while lifting so you have to make it perfect before you even take the weight off the rack.

When you set-up, make sure to take your time. Don't rush it. Even if you have to do your entire set-up multiple times, it is best to take that few extra seconds to get yourself in the best position to lift from, then rush it and risk missing a lift or getting injured.

Your set-up should be exactly the same every single time so that you are always lifting from the same perfect position and not just lazily going through the motions. If you want to bench BIG, then you need to take the time to perfect everything including your set-up.

GRABBING THE BAR TOO CLOSE OR TOO WIDE

Where you place your hands matters, because it effects how well you can transfer energy from you into the bar. To transfer the most energy, and have the strongest press, your elbows should be directly under your hands and in line with the bar when the weight is paused on your chest.

By grabbing the bar too wide, you are losing pressing power by taking the stress off of your triceps and putting it into your chest and shoulders. Though this decreases the range of motion you have to lift the weight, you are putting your shoulders in a compromised, and overall weaker position, that greatly increases the risk of injury.

Your shoulders are not designed to be pushed behind your back with heavy weight and elbows flared out to the sides. That is why we tuck the elbows slightly in towards our sides and raise our chest to decrease the stress placed on the shoulder joint. If this feels awkward to you, then practice closegrip bench press to help build up your triceps strength.

If you have shoulder problems that prevent you from getting your hands in closer, then check out my Mobility Exercises to work on improving your shoulder mobility and make sure you follow my How To Warm-Up Guide to help decrease pain and increase mobility before every workout.

By grabbing the bar too close, you are taking stress away from your shoulders and chest, and making your triceps work even harder. This is a great way to improve your triceps strength, but is not your strongest press. You want to use all of your pressing muscles to where they work most efficiently to have the strongest press.

Build your triceps strength by grabbing the bar slightly closer than normal, but test your strength by grabbing in the strongest position for you.

NOT TOUCHING THE BAR TO YOUR CHEST

This is one of the most common mistakes people who do not understand the bench press make.

Whether you are a gym bro, a bodybuilder or a powerlifter, it is NEVER correct to consider a partial bench press as a correct movement. There is a place for partial range of motion, but building complete upper body strength and muscular development does not come from half reps. Full range of motion is necessary for complete muscle growth and overall strength.

With that being said, it is really not that big of a deal if someone doing general fitness does a half rep, or bodybuilders stop a few inches off their chest. Unless you are competing for something that demands perfect form, who really cares? Focus on your form and just let them do their thing.

If you have shoulder problems or mobility issues that prevent you from touching the bar to your chest, then you should work on fixing these before progressing. It can be as simple as correcting your form to take the pressure off your shoulders, or may be an actual joint problem that needs to be attended too. Start by correcting your form, and if that does not fix it, do some mobility exercises to improve your shoulder mobility.

Also get my book *The Daily 30* to work on your bench press technique and shoulder mobility daily for the best results.

ARCHING TOO MUCH

This is a common mistake many people make after being taught to arch for the bench press. Arching is proper for the bench press, however, some people arch their lower back way too much.

The main reason for arching our chest in the bench press is to protect our shoulder joint. It is actually wrong to lay flat on the bench without arching, because this puts your shoulder in a compromised position and therefore neglects the safety of the lifter.

What is incorrect is over arching to where the arch is mostly in the lower back, not your thoracic (upper) spine. The goal should be to get your chest as high as possible, and not your stomach. Raising your stomach too much puts unnecessary strain on your lower back and decreases your leg drive.

Simply raise your sternum so that your chest is the highest point, not your stomach. For most people with a lack of thoracic (upper spine) mobility, this may be a very slight motion. If that is the case you should go through my How To Warm-Up Guide to help improve your arch and increase your overall pressing power.

OVER-TUCKING THE ELBOWS

It is important to tuck the elbows in towards your sides when benching to reduce the shoulder stress and give you a stronger press, but many new lifters over-tuck their elbows to where they come out of line from the hands. Your elbows should never be closer to your sides than your hands when tucking the elbows.

All you are doing is rotating your elbows in slightly so that they don't shoot out to the sides when you bring the weight down. This will also make the bar sit slightly lower on your chest.

If you don't understand what we mean by tucking your elbows, try to mimic it with dumbbells. Bring the dumbbells down with a neutral grip (palms facing each other), then press while rotating the dumbbells back to normal (palms facing towards your feet).

Just like the bench press, you are simply rotating your elbows in and out as you lift, so that they always stay in line with your hands. DO NOT let your elbows come out of line from your hands, wether using a barbell or dumbbells, because it will torque on your shoulders.

MOVING OR WIGGLING YOUR FEET

Moving, bouncing or wiggling your feet during the bench press is the same as if you were to do it during the squat. It shows that you are not tight and greatly decreases your lifting strength.

Your feet need to be stable during the entire lift. If they are constantly bouncing or changing position, then you are losing stability and leg drive. Whatever position your feet start in, they need to stay in that position.

Lock your feet into the ground, by pressing down while driving your toes to the front of your shoes, and stay there to maintain tightness throughout your entire body.

BOUNCING THE BAR OFF YOUR CHEST

DO NOT BOUNCE THE BAR OFF YOUR CHEST! We are here to build strength, not fake it! If you can't control the entire range, then you can't bench that weight!

You should always be in control of the weight and pause on your chest.

Pausing may be more difficult at first, especially if you are not used to it, but it makes you so much stronger than touch-and-go benching. For all your warm-ups, and whenever you are using <75%, try to work on pausing the bar on your chest for 1-2 seconds. Then as the weight gets heavier, you can use touch-and-go if you need it.

It is like saving and extra boost for when you need it. Still maintain control of the entire lift, but decrease the pause time as needed. That is how you get a brutally strong chest.

WRISTS BENT BACK

This is a common problem that is simple to fix, but takes time. You just have to focus on keeping your wrists straight, with the weight sitting at the base of your palm, during the entire set-up and lift, making sure to crush the bar in your hand. As your grip strength improves, so too will your ability to keep your wrists straight.

If you do not correct this, you will be losing a lot of pressing power and start to damage your wrists. Make sure to keep your hand, wrist and elbow all in line directly under the bar during the entire lift.

CHEST SINKS AS YOU LOWER THE WEIGHT

Your chest needs to stay high during the entire lift. If it sinks down as you lower the weight you are increasing the range of motion and putting strain on your shoulder joint. Both of these lead to a much weaker press.

As you lower the weight, keep your chest high by pulling the bar down with your back and sticking your chest out, the same as if you were doing a body row on a stable bar. Make sure that your shoulders stay tucked in and pulled together during the entire lift.

If you have tight shoulders, your chest may sink when the weight gets to a certain point due to a lack of internal rotation mobility. You can correct this by trying some mobility exercises and making sure you follow my How To Warm-Up Guide (see page 6) to get prepared before every workout.

TOP ACCESSORY EXERCISES

The best lift to build up your bench press is the bench press. That is the same for any lift. However, you can only bench so much and so often before you start overdoing it to where the benefits plateau. That is where accessory exercises come into play.

Accessory exercises allow you to get in more training volume and help to build up specific muscle groups that may need more direct attention.

For example, you can use closegrip bench press to build up your triceps strength or military press to build up your shoulder strength.

THESE ARE THE BEST ACCESSORY EXERCISES TO HELP YOU BENCH BIG:

- **Bench Press Variations** for different stimulus.

- **Military Press** for shoulder health and strength.

- **Dumbbell Press** for overall pressing power.

- **Weighted Dips** for triceps pressing power.

- **JM Press** for triceps strength.

- **Triceps Press Downs** for triceps strength.

- **Pull-ups** for back strength and shoulder stability.

There are thousands of other exercises that can help build up your bench press, but these are the most effective ones that have a direct carry-over to your bench press strength. Improve these, and your bench will absolutely go up!

These are also the accessory exercises you will be doing in any of my Mathias Method Strength Programs, including the 12 Week Bench Press Program in this book!

These exercises are hard, but they are also highly effective in building full body strength like nothing else can. Work these often and your strength will shoot up!

Lift variations allow for a different stimulus and can allow for new growth, building up specific parts of the lift. This is also a great way to target specific muscle groups that may be lagging behind and need more attention.

Variation can be simple or complex, but to build strength towards the main movements, it is important not to vary too far from the original lift. Start with simple variations before moving into more complex changes.

It doesn't make sense to vary the lift so drastically to where it is a completely different lift that may not have any carryover to your actual bench press.

HERE ARE SOME COMMON VARIATIONS YOU CAN USE TO SPICE UP YOUR LIFTS:

- **Hand Position**

- **Pauses**

- **Pressing Off Boards**

- **Specialty Bars**

- **Range of Motion**

- **Accommodating Resistance (Bands or Chains)**

- **Assistive Gear**

Also, bench press variations are a great way to spice up your training, but need to be limited. If you truly want to build a lot of strength, then you need to put in the work rather than just find ways to make the lift easier, or less boring.

Variation is best used with advanced lifters who have already mastered their lifting technique and progress is stalling. Beginners should rarely use variations in the main lifts if at all, because the best variation to build up your bench press is just doing more benching. It is only after standard benching is not working well that you should try something different.

Intermediate lifters can try some exercise variations infrequently, but most of the work should focus on perfecting the main lift.

How To Spot For The Bench Press

You should always bench press with spotters, and get a lift off no matter how light the weight is to you. This can actually make you stronger no matter what weight you are using, because getting handed the weight will allow you save energy and keep your shoulders locked in versus being forced to shrug the weight out over the hooks.

So if you are not training with a friend or two, you should be! They will help keep you accountable as you both fight through the tough training. Plus, they will be there when you need them!

If you do go to the gym alone, don't worry. Getting a spot for any lift is quit easy. All you have to do is ask!

Don't be shy either. If they are too busy, let them tell you that. Don't assume that they do not want to help, because most gym goers would be honored that you feel confident in them to help you. Just make sure you take a moment to asses the gym for potential spotters, if you don't have any on hand, to make sure you pick the right ones.

The Spotter

First, let's discuss what a "spotter"is. A spotter is someone that helps promote safety of the lifter by assisting the lift in case of a failed attempt.

If the lifter does not fail a lift or ask for assistance, then the spotter SHOULD NOT TOUCH THE WEIGHT!!! If a spotter does touch the weight, no matter the amount of assistance given, the lift is considered a failed attempt. No one finger help or taps, NOTHING!

Lifters should always use spotters, especially on lifts exceeding 80% of the lifters maximum and on sets in which the lifter gets close to failure.

Again, spotters are only there to assist in case the lifter fails. If the weight does not stop moving upward, then the spotter should not touch the weight, even if it is moving slowly.

All spotter assisted lifts DO NOT COUNT! Period! Exclamation point! Angry face!

CHOOSING YOUR SPOTTERS

When choosing spotters, it is best to choose people that are focused on your safety. They don't have to be very strong, because they do not have to lift all the weight. They just have to lift the extra 1-5% you can't. Your grandmother can spot you if you want! They just have to be focused on you and not staring at the girl across the gym.

You don't need the biggest, strongest or most experienced person to help you out. They are no use if they are not paying attention to your lift, or distracted with their own workout.

It is great to get people with a lot of experience, but it can also be really great to teach new lifters how to spot too.

Anyone can learn how to spot most lifts in a matter of seconds. Just explain what you are going to do and what you need them to do in case the worst happens. If they can understand what to do and be focused on the moment, then they are perfect! It can even be a great learning experience for them if they have not done it much before.

Just make sure that they know not to touch the bar unless the weight is about to fall on you!

THERE ARE 3 WAYS TO SPOT FOR THE BENCH:

1. **Main Spot (Hand Off)** - most common and best for lift offs, but safety depends entirely on the spotter.

2. **Side Spots** - very safe and highly recommended.

3. **Main and Side Spots** - most safe and preferred above all else if possible.

How To Hand Off

The Main Spotter stands at the head end of the lifter, both to hand the weight off and spot the entire lift.

A lift off is as simple as handing the weight to the lifter. You are not jerking the weight up and dropping it on them. You are simply handing it to them the same as you would with a 5lb. weight plate, just with a little more force. It should be a smoothly guided motion by both the lifter and spotter.

It is important that you are both on the same page before the lift off. Make sure that you have a routine or signal so you both lift the weight off at the same time. The most common way to do this is counting to 3. On 3, you both lift the weight into the start position, over the lifter's shoulders.

You, the spotter, should keep your hands grasped firmly onto the bar during the entire hand off and only start to slowly release your grip after the weight has stopped in position. Doing anything sudden can lead to disaster, so make sure the lifter has the weight before letting go.

You should then stay with the weight by guiding your hands about 1-3 inches below the bar during the entire lift. It is important that you do not touch the bar, making it a failed rep, unless the lifter needs help.

As soon as the lifter fails, do not assist with anymore reps. Grab the bar and rip it straight up, then back into the rack. Make sure not to pull the weight back into you before coming all the way up or you may miss the hooks and drop the weight on the lifter.

Also, DO NOT give minimal assistance to help them finish the lift. Either they get it, or they don't. Doing slowly guided reps does not build strength nearly as well as allowing the lifter to get the entire rep themselves. Simply rest and do another set instead.

How To Side Spot

Side spotters stand at each end of the barbell to lift the weight up in case of a failed lift.

This spotter should stand slightly in front of, or behind the weight plates on each side, close enough to grab the end of the barbell if needed. There can be up to 2 side spotters on each side of the barbell, but one on each side is most common.

The side spotter will need to move their hands with the weight, the same as the main spotter, leaving only 1-3 inches distance from grabbing the end of the barbell.

If the lifter fails the lift, it is very important the the side spotters lift the weight straight up with the lifter, and at the same speed as each other. You do not want one side coming up faster than the other making for a lopsided barbell.

Also, try to get spotters that are about the same height.

Having side spotters is very safe, but not necessary unless you are lifting over 400 lbs.

MAIN AND SIDE SPOTS

A combination of both a main and side spotters is the safest way to spot for the bench press. This ensures that the lifter is taking all necessary precautions to lift as safely as possible.

The main and side spotters perform their spots the same as described above. In case of failure, the spotters will all be there to assist.

If for any reason the bar slips out of the lifter's hands, all spotters should be there to catch the weight so that it does not fall on the lifter. This is uncommon, but can be fatal, so PAY ATTENTION!

You will see this style of spotting in all sanctioned powerlifting competitions and most powerlifting gyms that care for the lifter's safety. If you want to lift big numbers, this is the way to go with your spotters.

PART 3

BUILDING STRENGTH

12-WEEK BENCH PRESS PROGRAM

Maximize Your Bench Press Strength!

This program is based on the Mathias Method Strength System.

12-weeks. 12-weeks of hard work. That is all it takes.

During that time you will be significantly improving your bench press technique and building an incredible amount of strength. Both of which will have you more than ready to set a brand new PR!

However, it won't be easy. Over the next 12-weeks you will be taken on a journey that will lead you to something you have never done before. You will be pushed and tested every step of the way. You will learn new ways of building strength that you may have never learned otherwise and you will take your strength beyond what you may have ever imagined. When you are done, you will be changed and look back at where you used to be only to see how far you have come.

The only thing to do next is ask, "what's next?"! The answer, is up to you…

Note: This is a 12-week cyclical program that is meant to be done over-and-over again for as long as you wish. After completing a cycle, you can immediately start back over at week 1. However, I recommend you take 1-2 weeks between cycles to just go into the gym and have some fun doing workouts with less strict programming. This will give you a mental break from the strict programming and help you come back refreshed and ready for the next 12-weeks.

PROGRAM DETAILS

This is a 12 Week Strength Program that focuses on increasing your bench press max. In it I will guide you through the exact work you need to do in order to reach your new Bench Max!

This program can be used to repeatedly improve your bench press until your reach your goal of benching 300, 400 and even 500+ pounds! After you finish one 12 week phase, simply take a week off from benching and then begin again!

For many, this program may seem like a lot, but to bench more than before you have to put in more work than before. You have to do hard things, because hard things make you stronger.

This program is best for lifters with at least a year of bench press experience under their belt. If you have not been benching for that long or more, then you will benefit more from my *Base Of Strength Training Program* (see page 6), which is made to help you improve all 3 of your main lifts, simultaneously.

THIS PROGRAM HAS 3 PHASES:

1. **Volume Phase**

2. **Strength Phase**

3. **Max Phase**

Each Phase is 3 weeks long with every 4th week being a deload before starting the next phase.

PHASE 1 - VOLUME

The first 3 weeks of your training is the Volume Phase. This Phase will focus on increasing your total work capacity with light to moderate weight and a lot of volume.

This is the time to improve your technique and recover so that your body is ready for the more intense work ahead without becoming over fatigued.

This Volume Work is also used as a "Strength Reset" in which you give your body time off from maximal work to prepare it for more progress at your new found strength. This Phase is vital for your maximal strength, and will have your body craving more intense weights when complete.

DELOAD WEEKS

Every 4th week in this program is a deload and recovery week. This week allows your body to catch up on recovery, build up other weak areas and prepare you for the high intensity workouts the following week.

This is the time to focus on other accessory lifts, that will help to build up your body's weak areas and improve your overall strength.

Instead of Bench Press, your Main Lift for these weeks will be incline bench press. This is a great variation that has great carry over to the standard bench press, especially if you have relatively weak shoulders. Just remember to control the entire movement rather than bouncing the weight off your upper chest.

If you don't have an incline bench press you can sub it out for standing military press. This is also a great way to target your shoulders, but it doesn't have as much carry over to your actual bench press strength.

The intensity will be much lower on these weeks and you should not push yourself too hard. Just get in some work to improve your lift, but save most of your energy for the intense workout the following week.

Week 8 is another deload week, and is vital to allow your body enough time to recover fully before taking on your most intense workouts during your 4 week Peaking Phase!

PHASE 2 - STRENGTH

The next 3 weeks (5-7) are your Strength Phase. These workouts combine intensity and volume to build up the greatest amount of strength.

These workouts will be long and hard, but you will feel like a true Strength Warrior if you can get through them without being crushed by the weight!

Take your time with every set and make sure that you are moving with a purpose on every rep. Be in control of the weight, and do not let the weight take control of you.

PHASE 3 - MAX

The final 4 weeks, including your deload week, are what is called your Max Phase, or Peaking Phase. These workouts are designed to increase your maximal strength and prepare you to crush your Peak Week!

This is where you have your most intense workouts before backing off for at least 10-14 days in order to hit a Strength Peak where your body is ready to lift the most weight.

These 4 weeks are crucial to nail perfectly in order to peak at the right time and get the greatest improvement in your bench press max.

Make sure your recovery is on point and you do not do anything out of the ordinary during these 4 weeks.

PEAK WEEK

Peak Week starts with your Week 11 - Workout 1 and goes until your Max Day.

You will start Week 11 by working up to the heaviest weight that you feel you can do 2-3 clean reps with. This should be at least 90% of your old maximum, but can also be well over your previous 100% max, depending on how well the program has worked for you so far. This is going to be your heaviest workout of the cycle, but it is not meant for you to do an all time max. This is still a preparation for your max day, so save some.

When you find your perfect weight, you are going to do 5-10 singles with it, stopping when form begins to break down too much. If form breaks down before you reach 5 reps then you need to significantly drop the weight to where you can do clean singles. If you are working into a competition, then this working weight should be your opening lift.

This workout should give you a good idea of what your max should be on max day. If this workout goes well, then you can expect to hit 110% of this weight on max day. For example, if you were able to do 5-10 good singles with 275 lbs. then you can expect to bench 300+ lbs. on max day.

This is your last maximal workout before your max day and you should plan to max 10-14 days after this workout.

You will finish Week 11 off with your normal Base Work before moving to week 12.

Week 12 is also a deload week in which you will do minimal work and very low intensity for all of your lifts, so that your body is more than ready for Max Day.

You will start the week by doing only 5 sets of 3 reps at 50% of your max for Bench Press, followed by your normal Accessory Work. Keep your accessory work light and easy on this day and just get some movement in. You do not want to take the week off from lifting, but you also do not want to fatigue yourself with any of your workouts.

Keep all your workouts light and easy this week and have at least 1-3 days off from all training before max day.

MAX DAY

Max Day is your day. It is the day you have prepared for with every workout over the past 12 weeks. You are ready for this and you should wake up feeling super human!

Make sure that you are fully rested on the days leading up to your Max Day and your nutrition is on point. Stay hydrated and eat normally.

Do not try any new supplements or food protocols around this day. You don't need to be overly stuffed or caffeinated to lift heavy. You have been preparing for weeks and you are ready. Just go do it.

Take your time on Max Day. Take your time waking up. Take your time eating before hand. Take your time getting to the gym and take your time warming up. This is your day so let it last.

Warm-up slowly and take as long as you need between sets. As you get over 80% your rest should be between 5-10 minutes, not more or less.

Make sure everything is feeling good and move violently. If the weight is light, then it should look light. Drive into every rep as if it is your max and make sure your body is prepared to be explosive with that new max.

If you prepared properly, then this day will be easy for you.

When you are ready, go for it! Be confident in yourself and show the world WHO YOU ARE!!! It's Game Time! Go dominate!

Remember to tag @MathiasMethod when you post your new PR so I can see how you did!

If you want some good Game Day Motivation, then check out my motivation book *Motivated Mindset* (see page 6)! It will get you fired up for anything you pursue in your life no matter the challenges you face!

HOW TO MAX OUT PROPERLY

How you work up to your max can greatly effect your maximal strength. The goal is to stimulate your body for a maximal lift without over-fatiguing yourself to where you have major strength loss.

If you go in and do a bunch of unnecessary reps you are just going to be waisting energy. It is better to do more sets and less reps to conserve energy than try to do a full workout before hand. You wouldn't run a mile to warm up for a sprint, so don't make the same mistake here. All you need to do is feel the weight. When the weight feels good, move up.

Below we give you a common max out protocol, but you can add more sets if needed. Remember, the goal is to get your body prepared for maximal weight, and not fatigue you.

Take your time between sets and go when you are ready keeping the reps low. Remember to be explosive with every single rep as if it is a maximal lift.

- **Bar x 5-10**

- **30-40% x 5-10**

- **50-60% x 3-5**

- **70-75% x 3**

- **80-85% x 1-3**

- **90-95% x 1**

- **100-105% x 1**

- **105%+ x 1**

Add multiple sets as needed.

All percentages are based on your projected max calculated by your Week 11 - Workout 1 working weight multiplied by 110%. If you used 275 lbs. as your working weight for all 5-10 singles, then your projected max is 300 lbs.

If you had to lower the weight for that workout, then use the lower weight to calculate your projected max.

It is better to warm-up a little lighter than it is to warm-up going too heavy.

WEEKLY WORKOUT SCHEDULE

This bench program has you benching 2 times per week. Workout 1 is your Strength Work in which you will be improving your bench's maximal strength through intense training. Workout 2 is your Base Work in which you will be practicing your technique and increasing your overall training volume.

Your first workout of the week should focus on the lift you want to improve. In this case, that is your bench press. Make sure that you have at least 1 rest day before this training day, in which you do no gym or cardio work. That will allow you to be the most fresh and prepared to take on the challenging workout ahead.

The second bench press workout of the week should occur 3-4 days after your first bench press workout. It would also be best to have a recovery day before this training day, but it is not required. Just make sure that you are recovering enough.

All other workouts throughout the week should not include upper body presses of any kind. Avoid fatiguing your upper body on other training days, but you can use any training split you want.

This is the training split we have found most effective for this training program.

Day 1 - Bench Press Workout 1 (Strength Work)

Day 2 - Off

Day 3 - Lower Body Workout 1

Day 4 - Off

Day 5 - Bench Press Workout 2 (Base Work)

Day 6 -Lower Body Workout 2

Day 7 - Off

On all of your other training days, make sure that you do not push yourself too hard. If improving your bench press is your main focus, then save most of your energy for your bench days. Just get the work in that you need for other lifts and muscle groups to stay strong. Doing a 5x5 workout at about 70% with small 5lb. jumps every week should be enough to keep your other main lifts moving forward without over stressing your body. Or get my Squat and Deadlift programs to pair with this one! *(See page 6)*

#MathiasMethod   #BenchBIG

Follow @MathiasMethod on Social Media

and tag us in your #BenchBIG workout clips!

Also, feel free to reach out anytime with your questions

or technique checks!

Bench Press Workouts

Strength Work

The first workout of each week is your "Strength Work" in which you will focus on building maximal strength. This workout will have the heaviest lifts of the training week and require the most preparation and recovery.

Over the 12 weeks the intensity will vary to allow for optimal recovery between high intensity training sessions.

The first 3 weeks of each phase will have a gradual progression as you work up in weight, getting closer to your max each week. Then every 4th week is a deload week in which you will take a break from the intense lifting and work on other accessory lifts. This is the time where you can do a light variation of your main lift and work on a weak area. These 4 week phases get increasingly harder as you work towards your peak week.

Peak week is the last 10-14 days before your maximal lift attempt, starting with your first workout of week 11. It is crucial that you do this properly to get maximum results.

For your Maximal Work on week 11 you will work up to the heaviest weight you feel that you can do for about 2-3 reps, but make sure that you only do 1 rep. This should be at least 90%, but can also be well over your previous 100% max, depending on how well the program has worked for you so far. You are going to do 5-10 perfect singles with this weight, stopping only when you cannot perform the squat with reasonable form. Be careful not to push yourself too hard in this workout. You want to work hard, but not get injured before your max day.

After doing 5 or more singles with this weight, you can add a little weight, but no more than 3-5% if you feel good. If it is getting heavy during your first 5 singles, then maintain the same weight until form breaks down.

Week 12 is your official peak week where you will use very light weight and just work the movement. You want to stretch out the lift to allow for blood flow, but focus on recovery above all else.

Then, 4-7 days later test out your max by gradually working up in weight. Make sure that you get plenty of rest this week and only max out on a day that you feel ready, and not fatigued. Your other workouts during this week should also be light and easy.

BASE WORK

The second workout of each week is your Base Work. This is a light to moderately intense workout to help you get in more work while improving your technique.

For your Base Work you will be doing at least 5 sets of 5 reps with gradually increasing intensity. Most of the time you will be given a 5% range to work in. For this, work up to a weight within the range that feels good and moves well.

How you feel during these workouts will vary every week, so do not worry so much about the weight, even if you have to go lighter than expected. It is more important to focus on moving well and with perfect technique. Save the heavy stuff for your Strength Work days. Think of it as a movement and recovery workout.

As for your technique, since the weights are lighter for these workouts, every rep should be explosive and done with perfect form. Do not take it easy just because it is light. If it is light, then you should make it look easy by driving the weight up hard with every rep.

Also, for these workouts, only use equipment (belt, sleeves, wraps, etc.) if needed. Try to do every set 100% RAW, if you can. This will help increase your RAW strength and make you that much stronger when you do use equipment on other days.

Week 12 you will not have any Base Work as you prepare for Max Day. Use this as a recovery day.

PROGRAM CHART

WEEK	MAIN LIFT	SETS	REPS	% MAX	WEEK	MAIN LIFT	SETS	REPS	% MAX
WORKOUT 1 - STRENGTH WORK					**WORKOUT 2 - BASE WORK**				
1	Bench Press	5	5	70%	1	Bench Press	5	10	50%
2	Bench Press	5	5	73%	2	Bench Press	5	10	55%
3	Bench Press	5	5	75%	3	Bench Press	5	8	60%
4	Incline Bench Press	5	5	50-55%	4	Paused Bench Press	5	5	60-65%
5	Bench Press	6	4	77%	5	Paused Bench Press	5	5	65-70%
6	Bench Press	7	3	80%	6	Paused Bench Press	5	5	65-70%
7	Bench Press	6	3	83%	7	Paused Bench Press	5	5	65-70%
8	Incline Bench Press	5	5	55-60%	8	Paused Bench Press	5	5	70-75%
9	Bench Press	6	2	85%	9	Paused Bench Press	5	5	70-75%
10	Bench Press	5	2	87%	10	Paused Bench Press	5	5	70-75%
11	*Bench Press	5-10	1	*90% +	11	Paused Bench Press	5	5	65-70%
12	Bench Press	5	3	50%	12	**Bench Press**	*Max Day*		

*Week 11 - DO NOT MAX! Use the heaviest weight you can do 2-3 reps with for all 5-10 sets.

- **Weeks 1-4 and 8 (Workout 1)** - AMRAP the last set of bench press using the same working weight. AMRAP = As Many Reps As Possible *(always leave 1-2 reps in the tank and do not pause any reps)*.

- **Weeks 5-7 and 9-10 (Workout 1)** - Work up to a Daily Max of 1-3 reps after all your bench sets are complete. Work up slowly taking as many sets as needed, but do not reach failure. Just move something heavy. If the weights did not move well during your sets, then just do an AMRAP for your last set with your working weight instead.

- **DO NOT change your weights after achieving a new max during the program** - Depending on your experience level, you may very well surpass your old max when doing your daily maxes. This is expected and accounted for in the programming. Do not change anything.

- **Week 11** - DO NOT MAX OUT! Read the "Peak Week" section for details.

- **Always AMRAP the last set of bench on Base Work days, without pauses.**

All percentages are based on your current max before beginning the program, not your projected max at the end.

If you do not know your max, then do a low estimate. As in, something you know you can do 2-3 good reps with at the start of the program. You will actually get more out of the program if you go a little lighter than you need too versus going a bit too heavy.

WORKOUT 1 - STRENGTH WORK

Warm-Up:

The Daily 30	1-3 Rounds
Back Exercise	3-5 x 10

Technique Work:

Paused Bench Press (<50%)	3 x 5

Main Lift:

Bench Press	See Program Chart
*Overload Set	See Program Chart Notes

Accessory Work:

Dumbbell Press / Incline Dumbbell Press	5-10 x 6-10
Military Press / Dumbbell Military Press	5 x 5-10
Cable Press Downs	5-10 x 10-15
Face Pulls	5-10 x 10-15
Rotator Cuff Work (optional)	4 x 15-25
Hanging Leg Raises / Weighted Crunches	5 x 5-10
Mobility Work	10+ min.

*Done after your main work is complete, and <u>never to failure</u>.

Go to <u>MathiasMethod.com</u> for in-depth exercise descriptions.

WORKOUT 2 - BASE WORK

Warm-Up:

The Daily 30	1-3 Rounds
Face Pulls	3-5 x 10-15

Technique Work:

Paused Bench Press (<50%)	3 x 5

Main Lift:

Bench Press	See Program Chart

Accessory Work:

Incline Dumbbell Press	5 x 10-15
Dumbbell Military Press	5 x 10-15
Triceps Skull Crushers	5-10 x 10-15
Reverse Flyes	4 x 10-15
Lateral Raises	4 x 10-15
Rotator Cuff Work (optional)	4 x 15-25
Leg Raises / Crunches	5 x 10-15
Mobility Work	10+ min.

Go to MathiasMethod.com for in-depth exercise descriptions.

Rotator Cuff Work

The shoulder joint is the most movable joint in the body. Due to this, it is also one of the most common joints to injure.

Most shoulder injuries, and general pain, can be easily prevented and even cured just by simply taking some time to work on them.

Our shoulder is simply a stabilizer to pushing and pulling motions. However, most gym goers do way too many pressing exercises and not nearly enough pulling exercises. This puts the shoulder joint in a compromised position as it sits forward in the joint, misplaced and in pain.

To fix this, and prevent it, make sure that you are doing a lot of back work in the form of both vertical and horizontal rows. Also, make sure you are doing some direct rotator cuff work at least once per week to help improve your shoulder integrity and make for a stronger, more stable joint to press from.

Rotator Cuff strength is crucial for complete shoulder health. The rotator cuff musculature is composed of multiple small muscles that hold the shoulder joint into its socket. If these muscles are weak or out of balance then your shoulder health is compromised and you are at high risk for injury.

With this in mind, doing some shoulder mobility and rotator cuff work will allow for you to move better and get stronger.

Commonly, our shoulders have enough, or even too much, internal rotation strength and we need to increase the external rotation strength to help establish balance.

You should do your rotary cuff work AFTER (never before) your upper body pressing workouts or on off days, but never at the beginning of a pressing workout.

Make sure to control the entire movement and it is best to use a cable or band. Do not do these exercises just by holding a light weight plate or dumbbell. That does little to nothing for your shoulder and only trains your biceps.

Do 4 sets of 15-25 reps 1-2 times per week to keep your shoulders healthy.

WORKING THE ROTATOR CUFF

PURPOSE

Increase Rotary Cuff Musculature Strength, Improve Shoulder Integrity

PRIME MOVERS

Infraspinatus (Shoulder), **Teres Minor** (Shoulder)

To work the external rotators of your shoulder, you must go through an external rotation of the humerus, or upper arm bone, with appropriately added resistance. It is best to use a band or cable with light resistance to keep constant tension on the muscle.

Begin by grasping a band, or single cable attachment, with one hand. Have the band or cable anchored near hip height.

Go through multiple movements that include external rotation of the humerus such as with your elbow out horizontally from your shoulder to where you rotate your hand back over your shoulder, or to your side where you rotate your hand out laterally.

Work the rotator cuff from multiple angles. As long as you are externally rotating, you are working the rotator cuff.

WORKOUT DETAILS

All workouts and training protocols follow the Mathias Method Strength System Principles.

In the Mathias Method Strength System we don't train muscle groups. We train movements and base our workouts on improving one lift. This is because lifts like the squat, bench press, and deadlift are all full body lifts. They take your entire body working in unison to perfect and do not target one specific area.

By building up these powerful compound movements we will develop strength and muscle throughout our entire body.

We also believe in using only the most effective accessory exercises. Big bang exercises that build big muscle and big strength. Yeah, they are hard ones and they make you brutally strong too.

This training style may be different than what you are used to, but it is what has worked for me and countless others with the same goal of getting brutally strong.

The details of your training are discussed below.

THE WARM-UP

Warm-ups are just what you think. They are simply meant too, warm-up your body for the intense work ahead, not overly fatigue you.

If you are not used to doing some warm-up exercises before your main work, then it will be fatiguing at first until your body gets more conditioned. This is part of developing the work capacity to lift heavy weight, so do not skip this just because you do not feel like it. If you want to get stronger, you're gonna have to put in the work no matter how you "feel".

Warm-ups should be relatively easy and never done to failure.

Every workout you do should start with 1-3 rounds of *The Daily 30* (see page 6) to practice your movement patterns and improve mobility while you warm-up. This may seem unnecessary, but it will do wonders for your strength and help to alleviate any muscle or joint pain you have.

For both training days your first warm-up exercise will be a pulling exercise to help counteract all the pressing you are about to do. Back strength is actually one of the most important factors in providing strength for all of your lifts, which is why we have you start every workout with pulls to develop back strength.

Choose any back exercise that you feel helps you keep your shoulders healthy and back strong. It is best to do a horizontal row versus something like a cable pull-down, because of the angle of pull mimicking a bench press. Keep the weight moderate and really warm-up your back.

For added strength and performance, follow my How To Warm-Up Guide (see page 6) before every workout!

TECHNIQUE WORK

Exercise Technique is a crucial part of any movement based training program. Without proper technique your body will learn improper movement patterns that can hold back your strength and cause injury.

Technique is so important that it should be checked and improved every time you start a training session!

Your technique work is still part of your warm-up and therefore only light weights (<50% of your maximum) should be used to prevent over fatiguing yourself. The focus is on improving your movement pattern by utilizing perfect form, under controlled movements.

To develop more strength off your chest, we will use pause bench as your technique warm-up so you can get more time in that position. You will simply do your bench press as normal, pause at the bottom for 2 seconds, then explode back up without losing positioning. That will help to make the weak point of the lift your strong point for lifting BIG weight!

The main goals of this extra work is to prepare your body for the more intense work ahead, build up weaknesses and increase work capacity.

You should do only 3 sets of 5 perfect reps. Again, the goals are to improve the motion of this exercise and better prepare your body for the work ahead, not to pre-fatigue those muscles.

After completing your Technique Work, you are ready to begin your workout!

Start with your first exercise by doing the same number of repetitions you plan to train with for that day. If you are doing 3 reps for your working sets, do all your warm-ups with 3 reps. Start with a low intensity and work your way up slowly.

THE MAIN LIFT

The main lift, or main lifts, of any given workout, is the focus point of the session, where you put in the most effort. All of the training before and after the main lift is set to better improve this movement.

As this book is all about how to improve your bench max, bench press will always be your main lift for both workouts. One day per week they will be done at a high intensity with low reps to build maximal strength, while one day per week they will be done with a light-moderate intensity as you accumulate volume and practice technique, creating a higher potential for strength gain.

Together, varying between light, moderate and heavy loads will allow for continuous growth without stagnation.

Follow the 12 Week Bench Press Program Chart for your bench press sets, reps and intensity.

Always warm-up to your working weight slowly during each workout to fully prepare yourself for the work ahead.

BIG BENCH TIPS

For your main bench work, I recommend you pause all of your reps until it gets too heavy to do so. Touch-and-go is good for testing your strength, as long as you're not in competition, but pause bench is better for building strength. If you're like me, then after a while you will actually be stronger with pause press than a touch-and-go.

Also, the Bench Press is a triceps dominant lift, which means your triceps strength has the greatest carryover to your bench press strength. If you want a big bench, then you need strong triceps!

One simple thing you can do to greatly increase your triceps strength, above all else, is do all of your main work with a closer grip than normal to focus more on the triceps. Then when the weight starts to get heavy, or moves slow, you can widen your grip and get some extra power.

Just by simply making the lift a little harder, it will add that much more to your strength in the long run.

Now, you don't need to have a super narrow grip to focus on your triceps, and you don't want to vary too far from your normal grip or else your technique will be too far off. Simply just move each hand in no more than 1 inch to help put a little more stress on your triceps.

As you get towards the end of your sets, or start to work up in weight, widen your grip back to normal so that you still get plenty of practice in with your strongest grip.

OVERLOAD SETS

Overload sets are part of your Main Lift work on Strength Work training days. For this you will either do an AMRAP (as many reps as possible) set or work up to a Daily Max.

AMRAP

Weeks 1-4 and 8 - AMRAP the last set of bench using the same working weight.

For your AMRAP sets, do as many reps as possible minus one. We always minus one because we do not want to ever risk failure. It is better to save some for later, then grind with bad form or risk missing a lift, which stalls progress.

Also, don't pause any reps during your AMRAP set.

DAILY MAX

Weeks 5-7 and 9-10 - Work up to a Daily Max of 1-3 reps after all your bench sets.

A Daily Max is a near maximum lift for that given day. It is not a true maximum, because you are fatigued from all the previous work.

For your Daily Max, work up to something heavy, but do not push so hard that you lose technique or risk failure.

Depending on your experience level, you may very well surpass your old max when doing your daily maxes. This is expected and accounted for in the programming. Do not change anything.

DO NOT do any overload sets on weeks 11-12!

ACCESSORY WORK

Your accessory work is just a few hard hitting exercises to help build more strength and muscle throughout your entire body. You will be pretty exhausted by this point, but push through and take it as a mental challenge that will make you even stronger.

Your accessory work should be performed with moderate-intensity to allow for optimal muscle growth and proper technique. Always maintain good form to ensure proper muscle activation throughout the entire lift.

Focus on stimulating the muscle rather than just throwing around tremendous weight. It is important to always be in control of the weight.

Work every exercise hard and try to move up in weight when you can.

Make sure to finish off with some mobility work to prevent injury.

STRENGTH WORKOUTS

The accessory work for your Strength Work starts off with 5-10 hard sets of dumbbell press or incline dumbbell press. This is one of the best bench press accessory exercises you can do, because it mimics the bench press with more freedom of movement. This helps to build up your stabilizing muscles, plus you can change the angle of your hands to target different muscles and even increase the range of motion by letting your hands drop slightly lower than your chest.

You will follow that with a military press variation for shoulder strength. For both your dumbbell press and military press variations, you can switch between exercise variations week to week, or just focus on improving one each cycle.

After doing all that pressing work it will be time to directly target the most important muscle to increase your bench press…your triceps! You will do cable press downs to build both big and strong triceps ready to press BIG weight with ease. You have already done a ton of heavy tricep work with all your presses so this is a relatively easy triceps exercise to help finish them off for the day. Go moderately heavy and make sure you feel your triceps giving out before you move on to the next exercise.

Next up is face pulls. These are great for building your rear delts and upper back, counteracting all the pressing work you just did. These are very important for your shoulder health and need to be pushed hard. Put everything you have left into these to get your shoulders set back in place.

How many sets you do out of the 5-10 given for most of these exercises greatly depends on your your experience level and how much volume your muscles can tolerate. So, let your muscles be the judge, stopping only when they start to give out. If you are a newer lifter, 5 sets may be enough. If you are already a pretty big bencher, you may need all 10 sets. Just go until you feel it is time to move on.

Finish with some heavy ab work and mobility to keep your body looking and feeling good.

BASE WORKOUTS

For your Base Work accessories you will be doing a ton of dumbbell work to make sure both of your arms are getting built up equally. Dumbbells are very versatile and can help to hit your muscles from different angles while making your stabilizers work extra hard. This is extremely important for being able to bench BIG weight.

Remember, just because the weights are lighter or exercises are easier doesn't mean you should take it easy. This is not a rest day! Work every exercise hard and try to move up in weight when you can.

Start off with weights you can do at least 10 reps with for all 4 sets and try to increase the reps every week. When you can do 15 reps for all 5 sets then it is time to increase the weight and start progressing repetitions again.

Make sure to finish off with some ab and mobility work to prevent injury.

CARDIO/CONDITIONING

Conditioning, or cardio, is not necessary for this program, but can assist with dropping weight and improving recovery, if needed. Just DO NOT do cardio to warm-up!

Conditioning, is any form of work that improves your cardiovascular health and total work capacity while assisting with the goals of training. Some examples of conditioning are; jogging, sprints, jump rope, battle ropes, light circuit training, a daily WOD, sled dragging, or just manual labor.

Conditioning is meant to increase the ability for your body to withstand work and become stronger. If you have low cardiovascular health and little muscular endurance then the amount of work your body can withstand is greatly diminished, along with your ability to become stronger. So, if you have a low work capacity, you should add in conditioning until it improves.

Conditioning can be performed 2-4 times per week for 10-20 minutes at a time. You may utilize high intensity interval training (HIIT) or moderate intensity steady state training.

With high intensity intervals, work to rest should be at a 1:1 or 1:2 ratio. For moderate intensity steady state conditioning, the body should stay in motion throughout the entire time with little to no resistance in order to sustain a raised heart rate during the time used.

It is best to do conditioning immediately after all accessory work, just before mobility work. This will add to the work already done in the workout and allow for the greatest increase in muscular advancement.

Conditioning can also be done on non-training days if preferred, but should then be done for 20-30 minutes. Remember, conditioning is meant to condition your body, not break it down beyond what your body can repair before the next training session. Use relatively light loads and just keep moving.

MOBILITY WORK

Mobility Work is 10+ minutes of stretching at the end of every workout used increase flexibility, prevent injury and improve recovery. Focus on stretching out the muscle you just worked, or other tight areas.

It can be as simple as doing just 2-3 stretches for 2 minutes each to fix your elbow, shoulder, ankle, or hip pain.

Mobility work can also be replaced by yoga or any other activity that improves your body's ability to move as intended without pain, such as rolling out soft tissues.

It is best to mobilize right after a workout, but it can also be done on non-training days.

The goal is to get at least 30-40 minutes of mobilization done weekly to enhance your recovery and performance. That is just 10 minutes 3-4 times per week.

REST PERIODS

Rest periods between sets will vary for each part of the workout.

During your warm-up you can superset all your exercises together, as the intensity is not very high for these exercises, or you can take your time with each exercise to prevent fatiguing yourself too much before your main work. It is your warm-up, so do what works best for you.

For all your bench press work, or main lifts, rest as long as you need between sets, but realize that the longer you take between sets, the longer the workout will last due to the numerous sets.

Typically rest should be 2-3 minutes for loads less than 75% of your maximum and 3-5 minutes for anything heavier. You can take longer if needed, but don't waste all your time waiting to be ready. It is supposed to be hard and tiring, so push yourself and improve your conditioning if needed.

For all accessory work, rest 1-2 minutes between sets.

TRAINING TO FAILURE

There are 2 types of failure in training; technical and absolute.

- **Technical failure** is the point in which you can no longer perform a repetition with reasonably perfect technique. This commonly occurs 1-2 repetitions before absolute failure.

- **Absolute failure** is when no more repetitions can be completed without assistance.

It is good to know what failure feels like, but most of your work should be done with reasonably perfect technique to build the most optimal amount of strength.

You should really only reach technical failure on the last 1-2 sets of any workout, if at all. This means you reached maximal stimuli of the muscle fibers and central nervous system while still performing safe technique.

Reaching absolute failure too often will result in a much greater chance for injury and a much longer recovery period that may extend beyond the next training session. Not only that, but it teaches improper lifting technique as your body fights to lift the weight, and makes you weaker in the long run.

If you are training to failure, then you are training to fail!

The idea for strength training is too, accumulate volume for growth over multiple training sessions per week utilizing perfect practice. This will ensure safety while gaining the most amount of strength over time.

IF YOU DO FAIL

In training, your bench press sets should never go beyond technical failure during this entire program, excluding your Max Day. However, if you ever do fail a rep, then drop the weight by 10% multiplied by the number of reps you have left in your set and do the rest of your sets in shame.

For example, if you failed your last rep, then take off only 10%. If you failed on your 4th rep out of 5, then take off 20%.

If you complete the rest of your sets at this new weight with good form, then you can go back up in weight, but this decreased percentage is your punishment for not recovering properly. Shame on you! Just don't blame me for your lack of preparation.

Also, if the weight is effecting your technique too much and you are moving slow or out of position, then drop the weight by 10-20% until it looks better. It is your job to lift the weight properly and if you cannot do that, then your punishment is lifting lighter weight until you can get it right. Again, not my fault. Just do it right and make it look easy!

FINAL NOTES

- Things are going to go awry and that is ok. Not everything is going to go exactly as planned, and it will take time to perfect your bench press technique no matter your experience level. Just be patient.

- Just like anything else, whenever you try something new, such as changing your bench press technique, it will likely feel worse. Your body does not like change and the greater the change the worse things may feel. However, after practicing the new technique you will become so much stronger in the long run. Just trust in the technique and trust in the program. Practice and you will become perfect!

- Don't train lazy! If you do, you will develop bad habits that will haunt you for the rest of your lifting career! Don't squirm when you Bench, sit off to the side when you squat or shrug your deadlifts up. Make sure every rep is absolutely perfect and it will help you during your entire lifting career.

- Recovery is the most important thing! It doesn't matter what you do in the gym; if you can't recover from it, then you are not going to progress. Recovery is the only thing that is going to hold you back from making this program a success. So make sure you are getting enough sleep and fuel! That part is on you.

- Make sure you are doing your *Daily 30* to help with recovery and mobility throughout the entire program.

- Email me (ryan@mathiasmethod.com) with any questions!

- One more thing…

WOULD YOU DO ME A FAVOR?

Thank you for reading and I hope you learned a lot!

Before you go, please do me a HUGE favor and take a moment to let me know what you liked most about this book by leaving a review on Amazon! I read all my reviews and I love hearing how my work has helped others.

Plus, it helps more people learn what they can get from this book!

If you were not completely satisfied with the content of this book please let me know by emailing me directly and I will be happy to answer your questions or help you further.

Thank you, and keep getting stronger my friends!

Email: ryan@mathiasmethod.com

Do you know someone that would benefit from this book?

Please tell them about it!

Everyone can benefit from getting stronger!

MORE BOOKS BY RYAN J. MATHIAS

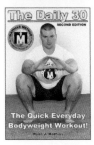   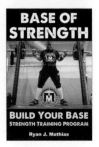

Available on

Amazon.com

and

StrengthWorld.store

STRENGTH
STRENGTHWORLD.STORE
WORLD

We have over 200+ articles on how to get stronger and workout properly, in and out of the gym!

Go to MathiasMethod.com to follow the Strength Blog and get all the awesome NEW Content we put out!

- **New Articles**

- **Workout Programs**

- **Valuable Strength Training Resources!**

FOLLOW US ON SOCIAL MEDIA

Facebook: @MathiasMethodStrength

Instagram: @MathiasMethod

Twitter: @MathiasMethod

YouTube: @MathiasMethodStrength

Reddit: u/mathiasmethod

Ironworks Gym

153 South Auburn St.

Grass Valley, CA 95945

PHONE #: (530) 272-9462

Home of the Mathias Method STRENGTH WARRIORS!

Thank you for allowing us to use your awesome facility to help make the world a stronger place!

Strength is only the beginning.

It is what you do with it next that really matters.

Printed in Great Britain
by Amazon

13061117R00054